First Teachers

The Barbara Bush Foundation for Family Literacy
Barbara Bush, Honorary Chairman

The mission of The Barbara Bush Foundation for Family Literacy is:

- to establish literacy as a value in every family in America by helping parents everywhere understand that the home is the child's first school, the parent is the child's first teacher, and reading is the child's first subject; and

- to break the intergenerational cycle of illiteracy by supporting the development of literacy programs that build families of readers.

First Teachers

A Family Literacy Handbook
for Parents, Policy-Makers,
and Literacy Providers

The Barbara Bush Foundation
for Family Literacy

Library of Congress Catalog Card Number: 89-83385
ISBN: 0-440-19805-4 (pbk)
ISBN: 0-440-19806-2 (trd)

Printed in the United States of America
First edition

  2 3 4 5 6 7 8 9 0

BOOK DESIGN BY MARIA CARELLA

Contents

Carol T. Powers THE WHITE HOUSE

Since the creation of The Barbara Bush Foundation for Family Literacy, many people have asked me: What *is* family literacy? Why is it so important? And what can we do to foster it? I am delighted to say that answers to these big questions can be found in this little book.

As you read through *First Teachers*, I hope you are as impressed as I was to learn that virtually every family literacy program discussed is the creation of a single determined and imaginative person. Individuals can and do make a profound difference in the lives of others, and the stories of these programs stand as an inspiration to action for each of us.

Above all, *First Teachers* is meant to be useful. It clearly illustrates some of the most promising ways to help adults help their children and themselves to literacy. All who want to get involved with family literacy programs can profit from the real and varied experiences presented here.

First Teachers represents the contributions of generous and gifted people, not the least of whom are the staff and students of the programs described. It is our hope that this book will show that there are many exciting routes to the goal of making literacy a value in every American family.

Acknowledgments

The work and support of a number of individuals have made this publication possible. First, we would like to acknowledge the important role played by the Association of American Publishers (AAP), under the leadership of their president, Ambassador Nicholas Veliotes, who marshalled the resources to publish this book. In particular, we would like to thank Lawrence Hughes, chairman of the board of AAP and chairman of the Hearst Trade Book Group, Alberto Vitale, secretary of the board of AAP and president, chief executive, and chairman of the board of Random House Inc., and Jack Hoeft, president and chief operating officer of Bantam Doubleday Dell Publishing Group, Inc., for their generous help.

Benita Somerfield, president of Simon & Schuster Workplace Resources and executive director of The Barbara Bush Foundation for Family Literacy, was responsible for the development of the text from materials submitted by the programs as well as for project oversight. Special thanks go to Karl Haigler, special advisor for literacy to the governor of Mississippi, who developed the Program Summary Chart; Doris Gunderson, the foundation's executive assistant, who compiled the Additional Sources of Information and Assistance; and to Lisa Drew, vice-president and senior editor, William Morrow & Company, Inc., who contributed her editorial expertise to the project.

Finally, we would like to thank Susan Porter Rose, Chief of Staff to Mrs. Bush, for her guidance and support.

Introduction

The Problem

Not long ago, the fact that tens of millions of America's citizens have serious basic skills deficiencies was unknown to the general public. Today the magnitude of the literacy problem and the consequences it could have for our nation's economic competitiveness, our democratic traditions, and even our national defense are frightening realities to businessmen, policy-makers, the media, and the general citizenry. The statistics are sobering:

- Almost one million students drop out of high school every year. (U.S. Department of Education)
- Only a small percentage of high school graduates have the reading, writing, and reasoning skills they need to function optimally in society, to achieve their goals, and to develop their knowledge and potential. (National Assessment of Educational Progress)
- More than 80 percent of our post-secondary institutions now provide remedial basic skills courses to high school graduates so that they are able to function in regular classes. (*The Condition of Education*, 1986)
- 36 percent of Fortune 500 service and industrial companies offer employees remedial courses in reading, writing, and reasoning. (*Business's Response to Education*)
- More than three-fourths of those entering the nation's work force between now and the year 2000 will have limited verbal and writing skills, which will be suited to fewer than half of the jobs being created. There is a looming "skills gap." (*Workforce 2000*)

These basic skills–deficient adults are not just citizens and workers in our society. Many of them are parents as well, and there is a growing body of research that indicates literacy correlations between parent and child. For example, the level of parental education, particularly that of the mother, is a strong factor in predicting the literacy proficiency of children

1

and young adults. (National Assessment of Educational Progress, 1985) Findings such as this have laid the groundwork for the development of family literacy programs to attack the cycle of illiteracy that often remains unbroken from generation to generation.

"Because of this intergenerational effect of the parents' education on the child's, it is unlikely that we will be able to make a major difference for the child unless we place equal priority on education and academic remediation for the parent." (*Toward a More Perfect Union,* Ford Foundation, February 1988)

Family Literacy:
A response with potential for success

With some exceptions, the traditional response to the nation's literacy problems has been a two-track system of both public and private-sector programs; a *remediation* track for the adult in the form of adult literacy education or, more recently, workplace literacy programs; and a *prevention* track for the child through early intervention efforts, such as the Head Start program. Tom Sticht analyzes the results of these traditional efforts in his thought-provoking report, *Making the Nation Smarter: The Intergenerational Transfer of Cognitive Ability.*

Family literacy programs approach the problem somewhat differently. Although there is no single definition or single "family literacy model," these programs operate on the stated or implicit belief that it is important for the parent or primary care-giver to place a high value on the acquisition of literacy skills and to take an active role in the child's education in order for that child to do his or her best at school. Further, the more literate that parent or care-giver becomes, the more effective he or she will be in performing the necessary at-home and school-related tasks that support the child's educational development.

A rich mixture of programs—some public, some private, many public/private partnerships—currently exists in diverse settings around the country. Most of them are quite new (one to five years old). (State and local family literacy efforts also have received support over the past five years from a variety of federal programs. See pp. 68–70.) Ruth Nickse, developer of the now defunct Collaborations for Literacy, one of the more promising early efforts, has written an informative paper for the U.S. Office of Educational Research and Improvement entitled "The Noises of Literacy: An Overview of Intergenerational and Family Literacy Programs," which reviews the history, the research base, and the status of these intergenerational efforts in depth.

First Teachers presents annotated "snapshots" of ten of these pioneering and promising efforts. Almost every program was begun by an individual with a vision of a new way to solve a demanding educational problem. The chart that follows their stories summarizes the key features of each program: goals, target population, outreach techniques, funding sources, support services, materials used, special features, and outcomes. Common interests, creative approaches, and differing goals are apparent, as is the anecdotal, informal nature of evaluation techniques that most of these relatively new programs use to measure outcomes.

Above all, these family literacy programs, as well as hundreds of other pioneering efforts around the country, reflect the belief that the role of the parent in the educational development of the child is critical—that parents are a child's first and most influential teachers. If this is true, it follows that intergenerational approaches to solving the nation's literacy problems make sense. The goal of this book is to support and encourage such efforts.

Family Literacy:
Programs & Practices

PARENT AND CHILD EDUCATION (PACE) PROGRAM

PACE—Laura Embry, 1989

Theresa was married at thirteen, had her first child at fourteen, and had three more children before she was twenty-four. Her own mother had dropped out of school early to have children. Theresa had attempted to get her high school equivalency diploma (GED), but circumstances made it too difficult. Theresa's husband had also left school when they were married and was not enthusiastic about her desire to go back. Theresa had to convince him she could take care of their home, children, and him if she went back to school. She did all of that and more. She was astounded at her rapid success in the Parent and Child Education program and expressed great pleasure at what the program had done for her and her daughter. As Theresa put it, "It pleased me to see what she could do with her mind, how she could learn so much. I went as much for her as for myself."

Background

Two Kentucky educators, one an expert in adult education and the other an expert in early childhood education, shared a 120-mile daily commute to work. The latter, Jeanne Heberle, believed that early childhood education was the key to raising Kentucky's low literacy levels; the other, Sharon Darling, believed that the best hope was in remedial help for those adults who would parent the next generation. Out of this amiable bickering came the idea for the Kentucky Parent and Child Education (PACE) program, winner of a 1988 Innovations prize given by the Ford Foundation and Harvard University's John F. Kennedy School of Government. One of ten winners selected from 970 applicants, PACE is the first literacy venture using state funds to serve parents and children at the same time in public school.

This innovative idea became a reality in 1986 when Roger Noe, chairman of the Education Committee of the Kentucky House of Representatives and a former literacy volunteer, aggressively supported and ultimately helped pass legislation that provided $300,000 to open six centers on a pilot basis in the first year and $900,000 to triple the scope of the program in the second year. In 1988, the project received an additional $1.8 million to continue through 1990.

The Program

Setting: PACE is administered by the Kentucky Department of Education and is offered in eighteen classrooms in twelve Kentucky school districts—Bell, Butler, Estill, Fleming, Hart, Letcher, Owsley, Magoffin, Metcalfe, Monroe, and Spencer counties, and Harlan Independent. Most school districts provide space in local schools for PACE classes, but three districts use neighboring locations.

Funding

$800 a year per participant (State funds).

Components

Parent literacy training: Adults receive training in basic language and math skills and social studies. Those with adequate academic skills receive instruction to prepare for the high school equivalency (GED) tests.

Parenting/parent education: Adults take parent education courses. At scheduled times they participate in classes with their preschool children and help their children learn. The two generations share meals and playtimes.

Prereading/language development activities: Parents and children are involved separately and together in emergent-literacy activities. For example, parents read simple books to children to help improve their own reading and to help children develop thinking skills and a love of reading. Children attend an on-site preschool program.

Other: Parents are encouraged to serve as educational role models for their children. Employability and general life-skills development are encouraged along with a love of learning.

Evidence of Success

- 70 percent of the adults either received GED diplomas or raised their grade levels by at least two years on a standardized reading test.
- Participants report a better understanding of their children's abili-

7

ties and needs as well as a newly acquired belief that their children could succeed in school with *their* help.

- PACE preschoolers exhibit measurable developmental gains. Classroom teachers can see the difference when PACE children enter their classes.

Advice to Policy-Makers and Practitioners

- Provide extensive training for staff and supervisors. Train adult education teachers in the principles of the early childhood and parents' time curriculum, and train the early childhood teachers in the principles of adult education curriculum.
- Responsibility for planning the parents' time with the children should be shared between the two teachers, i.e., early childhood and adult education.
- Anticipate recruitment problems and develop practical solutions. For example, offer child care for children not in the program, and home-based instruction to overcome parents' initial shyness and lack of confidence.
- Maintain direct local administration and supervision. This results in their commitment to the program and maintains the regional characteristics necessary for the comfort of the participants.

THE KENAN TRUST
FAMILY LITERACY PROJECT

Kenan—Vera Gatano, 1989

"When I heard about this program I didn't think I would be able to go back to school, with all my problems. But the staff came to my home, and they made me so at ease that I felt that whatever happens, I can do it. I always wanted my GED, and this program provided meals, transportation, and a program for my child. Social Services let me count the program instead of going to work. That was encouraging, and I just ran out of excuses . . .

". . . The most important thing about the program was having R.L. with me. I didn't feel bad about leaving him with somebody while I did something for me. We were together. I wouldn't have been able to come if R.L. had not been included, and even if I could have come, I probably would not have come without him. I thought I might have done something after all my children were in school . . .

". . . In the future I will be reading more with him. Before we came into this program I read to him sometimes, but not regularly. I'll keep books and materials around in case he wants some. I thought that children didn't learn until they started kindergarten, so that's when you started trying to teach them, but now I know ways to help him learn now. It's not like teaching, it's more like playing. I learned to be a teacher from him. I've learned that he can learn now."

—Regina
(case study of a student,
transcribed from audiotape)

Background

The back country of Kentucky is not typically a place in which people come to look for innovative ideas in education; however, that's where William C. Friday, former president of the University of North Carolina system, and Thomas S. Kenan III, both of whom represented the William R. Kenan, Jr. Charitable Trust, first observed the PACE program in action and met Sharon Darling. They had been referred there by the then U.S. Secretary of Education, William Bennett, who had been introduced to Ms. Darling and her ground-breaking work by his Adult Literacy Initiative director, Karl Haigler.

Friday and Kenan observed the program for an entire day, and returned home moved by the personal testimony of adults and children alike and convinced by the evidence that the program had an excellent chance of breaking the cycle of illiteracy.

The Kenan Trust Family Literacy Project began on a small scale in March 1988, with two sites in Louisville, Kentucky. By that fall, there were three sites in Louisville and four in North Carolina. The model will be replicated in ten additional states by August 1989.

In the spring of 1989, the growing national interest in family literacy as an educational strategy, the popularity of the Kenan model, and the demand for help in setting up and running Kenan programs motivated the Trust to give Ms. Darling a grant to establish the National Center for Family Literacy (see page 68). The center enrolled its first trainees, from eleven states, in August 1989 and already has a growing waiting list.

The Program

Setting: The projects are located in elementary schools. Two full-size classrooms are needed for each client group. The sites are as follows:

North Carolina
    Teresa C. Berrien Elementary School
    Fayetteville, NC
    Coordinated between:
    Cumberland County School System
    Fayetteville, NC, and
    Fayetteville Technical Community College
    Fayetteville, NC

    Walnut Elementary School
    Marshall, NC
    Coordinated between:
    Madison County School System
    Marshall, NC, and
    Asheville-Buncombe Technical Community College
    Asheville, NC

    Gregory Elementary School
    Wilmington, NC
    Coordinated between:
    New Hanover County School System
    Wilmington, NC, and

Cape Fear Community College
Wilmington, NC

Carver Elementary School
Henderson, NC
Coordinated between:
Vance County School System
Henderson, NC, and
Vance-Granville Community College
Henderson, NC

Kentucky

School sites are coordinated with the Jefferson County school system and are located in:

McFerran Elementary School,
Louisville, KY

Roosevelt-Perry Elementary School
Louisville, KY

Schaffner Elementary School
Louisville, KY

Funding

Privately funded by the William R. Kenan, Jr. Charitable Trust, each program costs $45,000.

Components

Parent literacy training: The parent education curriculum focuses on the special needs of undereducated adults, some of whom are nonreaders, some almost ready to take the GED exam. While individualized learning programs are an important part of the three-hour block, the teacher serves as a small-group facilitator, discussion leader, and coach much of the time. Adult students are encouraged to set their own goals and assist the teacher in the selection of materials and methods to meet those goals.

Parenting/parent education: Curriculum developers set aside two specific times in the school day to address the needs of "at risk" parents, those who are unfamiliar with the responsibilities and joys of interacting with their children. Parent Time (PT) is usually scheduled for forty-five minutes after lunch, while the children are playing outside. Discussions based on high-interest topics selected by both parents and teachers highlight aspects of nurturing, disciplining, and communicating, as well as accessing community resources. PT serves as a unifying event that solidifies the group and encourages attendance and retention.

Parents as Teachers (PAT) joins the preschooler and parent in activities that stimulate interaction and reinforce the benefits of involvement. Parents learn how to teach while playing with their children, but they are encouraged to let the child lead the play period. The children love this part of the day, when the parent's complete attention focuses on the child.

Prereading/language development activities: Prereading/language development activities are centered on the curriculum, which encourages children to initiate the learning experiences through participation in activities they plan and carry out themselves. The active learning builds on the children's existing strengths and accomplishments.

Other: While their children nap, the parents study preemployment skills, such as goal setting, self-esteem, interviewing, and job readiness. At other times, the adults perform volunteer jobs within the school, such as tutoring, reading a story to a class, and working as library or kindergarten aides. These jobs help them feel comfortable with the school staff—both teachers and administrators—and help the school staff better relate to parents, who often do not take part in school activities. These jobs also serve as work experiences for the parents and later as references when they seek employment. Some of the parents have been hired to work in the schools upon their completion of the program.

Evidence of Success

- Parents and their children express significant gains in establishing a more positive self-concept and independence.
- Staff and parents describe important changes in language, decision-making, and preacademic performance of their children.
- Adults functioning at GED level when entering the program have completed the GED requirements.
- Children who were in programs long enough to expect results made

significant gains in behaviors assessed by the curriculum documents.

Advice to Policy-Makers and Practitioners

- Form an advisory committee of persons who can relate well and with some authority to clients, the general community, service-agency personnel, and resources for the program.
- Select a staff that will commit itself to work as a team for the goals and ideals of the program.
- Determine the range of needs that can be addressed within the project site and limit enrollments to the clients who can be served most effectively. The greater the diversity, the smaller the number that can be served well by a staff.
- Assign adequate space to both the early childhood and adult literacy components of the program and reserve them exclusively for those purposes.
- Integrate the project staff into the school.
- Find meaningful tasks within the school that parents can select to work as volunteers.
- Recruit clients before the program is expected to start.
- Have the equipment, supplies, and materials on hand as programs begin.
- Support the staff when they seem to be burdened by the problems facing the parents and families.
- Continue to reinforce the goal of family development, and let neither the adult education nor early childhood development goals outweigh the primary goal.

SER FAMILY LEARNING CENTERS (FLCs) OF SER-JOBS FOR PROGRESS, INC.

SER—Allison Parker, 1989

When Luisa went with her friend to the local SER program, she had no intention of enrolling herself. Nevertheless, a SER counselor convinced her that she could learn English and eventually get a job outside of the house. What made the idea even more appealing to Luisa was that she was eligible to bring her five-year-old son, Cesar, with her to the SER Family Learning Center. This way he could be nearby, learning along with her.

Cesar blossomed before her eyes, Luisa said. "He loved working on the computers and I knew that the things he learned would give him a head start when he started school."

As Cesar progressed in his basic academic skills, so, too, did Luisa in her proficiency in English.

"At first it was difficult, but the computers really helped. I had the hardest time learning verb tenses, and no matter how much time my instructor spent with me, I just couldn't get it," she said. "When I started working on the computers, it all fell into place and I finally understood them. It was so exciting!"

—From a case study of a
29-year-old mother of two

Background

SER-Jobs for Progress was founded in 1964 as a voluntary community-based organization. It presently operates 111 programs located in eighty-three cities throughout the United States. SER programs place special emphasis on the needs of Hispanics in the areas of education, training, employment, business, and economic opportunities.

Since 1986, when the board of directors decided that literacy training and basic remedial education should be the primary service for participants, SER National has been implementing its Hispanic literacy initiative through the Family Learning Center (FLC) concept.

The FLC has three components: Basic and Job Skills Training, Literacy Councils, and Intergenerational Enriched Child Care. SER provides literacy training, GED, vocational skills, employment skills, and parenting and health education to adolescents both in and out of school, welfare parents, and senior citizens. Preschoolers, in addition

16

to receiving social, cultural, and health-related services, spend at least one hour per day using educational technology and software. SER-Jobs for Progress, Inc., is sponsored by the League of United Latin American Citizens (LULAC) and the American G.I. Forum, the two oldest and largest Hispanic organizations in the United States.

The Program

Setting: The SER literacy campaign focuses on the establishment of forty local SER corporation training facilities in fourteen states and the District of Columbia. About twenty of these FLCs have either been installed or are in the process of being established in SER training facilities. Three have programs to which parents bring their children for instruction. These children's programs are called SER-Care and are located in facilities in Dallas, Texas; Milwaukee, Wisconsin; and Providence, Rhode Island. Thirteen other sites had been targeted for SER-Cares as of May 1989.

Funding

SER receives programmatic grants from the U.S. Departments of Labor, Education, and Health and Human Services, and from private sector financial and in-kind contributions. Local SER Corporations are funded, among others, by the federal, state, county, and city branches of government, as well as by the private sector. Most federal monies are awarded through state Job Training Partnership Act (JTPA) programs.

Components

Parent literacy training: Automated learning environments are supplemented by print and videotape materials. Certified teachers lead the classes.

Curriculum includes instruction in literacy skills, English as a second language, basic adult education, high school equivalency preparation, advanced math and science, life-coping skills, job-search/work-coping skills, and health education (including AIDS and substance abuse).

Parenting/parent education: Curriculum includes prenatal care, infant nutrition, hygiene, bonding, basic obstetric and gynecological checkups, child development, and methods for effective intellectual and motor stimulation.

Prereading/language development activities: Preschool children work in five major areas to help them learn the alphabet and associate sounds with letters: computer-aided instruction, writing in journals, reading along with recorder cassettes, writing/typing, and making words with such materials as crayons, clay, and pipe cleaners.

Other: Many affiliates provide vocational-skills training in such areas as beginning and advanced office automation, advanced technology, automotive maintenance, and nursing assistance.

Evidence of Success

- More adult participants are active in their children's education. They develop increased interest in sharing and monitoring their children's homework and study time.
- Adults are motivated to learn more so that they can keep up with their children's educational development.
- Many adults obtain GED credentials as a result of SER's instructional program.

Advice to Policy-Makers and Practitioners

- Practitioners must be highly skilled, sensitive to the problems of racial and ethnic minorities, and willing to work hard to carry out the program.
- Avoid single sources of funding, which may restrict literacy service. Look for diverse funding sources, providing flexible dollars that encourage innovation.
- Target a particular population. Don't attempt to be the solution to the national problem.
- Don't restrict the program to an exclusive automated learning system or technology. Addressing the problems posed by illiteracy requires ongoing enhancements and incorporation of the latest developments in technology.
- Listen to experienced educators when choosing materials. Don't believe everything you read and hear from vendors.

PARENT READERS PROGRAM

Parent Readers Program—Martha Leigh, 1989

"Last summer there was a big thunderstorm. Everybody was frightened. I remember some things I read in a book. . . . We all sat together in the room, really scared at the noisy, heavy rain. . . . We started reading. It was really fun. They started asking questions, where lightning comes from. I said I can't really explain to you but I have a book that will give you the answer."

—Serafine R.,
student

"I'm strengthening her mind when I'm reading to her. And believe it or not, I think when I'm reading to her, I'm also learning. Even if it's a simple story, I'm getting something out of it. . . . It's like I'm building my vocabulary even if it's simple words. I'm building her vocabulary too. Sometimes when I'm reading to her, I'll explain something in my own words, using a word that's maybe a little too big and she'll ask what the word means. And I'll tell her. And she'll use the word."

—Madeline G.,
student

Background

Designed and developed by Ellen Goldsmith, Ed.D., and Ruth D. Handel, Ph.D., the Parent Readers Program at New York City Technical College of the City University of New York is an ongoing intergenerational literacy project that seeks to create families of readers. It offers a workshop series for adults in which children's literature is used to teach parents how to read and how to discuss books with their children at home. The classes consist of first-generation college students enrolled in remedial reading courses and their pre-school and school-age children.

Following a survey of home reading activities and attitudes, a pilot project was launched in spring 1987 to test the appeal of such workshops (Would students come? Would they respond enthusiastically to children's literature?) and to determine whether participants' concern for their children would translate into efforts to help them become better readers. (Would students learn reading comprehension strategies? Would they read to their children at home?) The pilot workshops drew thirty-three enthusiastic participants.

Many of the students had not been read to as children; Drs. Goldsmith and Handel read stories aloud to them so they could enjoy and learn the read-aloud process.

At the end of these pilot sessions the participants selected books as gifts for each child in their household. As they left, many students requested that the workshop series be continued.

The Program

Setting: The program is housed in New York City Technical College, an urban community college in downtown Brooklyn that is part of the City University of New York. At present, about 75 percent of the students are required to take remedial classes in reading, writing, and/or mathematics, and about 80 percent receive financial aid.

The program design has been replicated in other settings as well: The Partnership for Family Reading, a collaboration of Montclair State College and the Newark, New Jersey, public schools, attracts parents for workshops in reading to their children, borrowing books for home use, and discussing books with their children. Located in seven elementary schools, the partnership serves approximately two hundred students and is supported by foundation funding. The partnership is directed by Ruth D. Handel, a founder of the Parent Readers Program. Teacher training is an additional element.

Funding

An initial grant of $10,000 from the Taconic Foundation supported the development of the program. A $10,000 grant from the Robert Bowne Foundation supported curriculum development and the following grants have supported the continuation of services: A $50,000 grant from the Vincent Astor Foundation, a $60,000 grant from the Aaron Diamond Foundation, a renewal grant of $10,000 from the Taconic, a $3,000 grant from New York Telephone, a $3,000 grant from the Morgan Stanley Foundation, a $3,000 grant from the New York City Technical College Foundation, a $650 award from the City Tech Fund for Excellence.

In addition, two research awards from the office of the provost of New York City Technical College supported program evaluation, and the generous donations of children's books from numerous publishers have been an invaluable resource to the program.

Components

Encouraged by the students' enthusiasm and level of participation, Goldsmith and Handel developed a children's literature curriculum with parallel adult selections, keying both to appropriate reading-comprehension strategies. A six-stage model was developed for the workshop format. Components of the model are:

I. Introduction or Sharing of Reading Records

Participants share two types of records of books read in the program. The children's reading record is a form on which parents list the books they have read to their child at home and include brief comments on the child's reactions. The books, related to the genre or topic of each workshop, are borrowed from the program. The adult reading record, tailored to each workshop, monitors students' abilities to apply the reading strategy to adult selections related to the specific workshop topic or genre.

II. Introduction of Type of Book and Reading Strategy

A different type of book is presented at each workshop.

First, a brief description of the characteristics of the genre is given, along with examples of books appropriate for different age groups.

Second, an initial presentation of the reading strategy is made, and is further explained by applying it briefly to several of the books.

Charts listing the characteristics of the genre and steps of the strategy are displayed.

OVERVIEW OF WORKSHOP CONTENT

Semester	Type of Book	Reading Strategy
Fall 1987	Picture Books	Asking Questions
	Social Studies Books	Learning New Information
	Folktales	Making Predictions
Spring 1988	Fables	Drawing Conclusions
	Books about Science	Learning New Information
	Poetry	Rereading
Fall 1988	Family Stories	Making Predictions
	Informational Books	Learning New Information
	Poetry	Rereading
Spring 1989	Informational Books	Learning New Information
	Fiction	Making Predictions
	Poetry	Rereading

III. Demonstrating the Reading Strategy

Experience has shown that participants need to see the strategy in operation, since it usually will be unfamiliar to them and not part of their reading behaviors, either for their own adult reading or in reading to their children. The instructor demonstrates that strategy by going through the steps while reading a book or a selected number of pages aloud. Students may be invited to participate with the instructor.

Strategies have included asking questions, making predictions, drawing conclusions, learning new information, and rereading.

IV. Practicing the Reading Strategy

To consolidate learning, participants practice the strategy themselves. In pairs, with one assuming the role of parent and the other the role of child, participants take turns reading aloud and going through the steps of the strategy.

V. Adult Reading

The goal is for participants to apply the reading strategy to adult reading selections. To accomplish this, parallel adult selections on the same topic as the children's literature have been chosen; the interest and excitement evoked by the children's book provides motivation and background information for the more difficult adult reading.

The following activities take place:

- Discussion of ideas and information from the children's selection to provide a bridge to the adult selection.
- Discussion of ideas or information related to the adult selection.
- Distribution of the adult reading selection and its accompanying adult reading record with review of the active reading strategy and suggestions of ways to apply it to the adult selection.

VI. Book Borrowing

The child's reading record is distributed, and participants select books to read to their children at home.

VII. Family Read-Aloud Celebration

Another feature that was added to the program as a result of information obtained from the pilot phase is a family read-aloud celebration at the end of each workshop series. This event allows participants to meet one another's children and to engage in book browsing, book reading, and book selecting activities in a relaxed and festive atmosphere. At this event, families read together.

Evidence of Success

Changes in the literacy environment of the home are attributable to the program and are confirmed by program evaluation data. Parents now:

- Involve children in reading activities.
- Try to teach reading behaviors and attitudes that they experience in the workshops.
- Become sensitive to factors that can affect a reading relationship with the child, such as pinpointing his or her interests, disposition, and developmental needs.
- Serve as reading role models by demonstrating the importance of reading in their own lives.
- Become literacy resources by providing more opportunities for reading, such as encouraging library visits, bringing books home from the program, and reading to neighborhood children.

Advice to Policy-Makers and Practitioners

- This program is labor intensive, so if it is being initiated without a great deal of financial and personal resources, start small.
- Recruit actively. Use past participants as recruiters, send letters after an initial show of interest, make follow-up phone calls, develop personal contacts.
- Provide incentives to participants. Possibilities include books as gifts, family reading celebrations, certificates of participation for parents, refreshments at workshops.
- Get outside publicity for the program. It not only helps to keep the program attractive to funders but also provides validation for the participants.
- Be flexible. The model can be applied to a variety of settings. The constants are the interactive nature of the workshops and the accessibility of children's literature. The use of adult readings, the length of the sessions, and the number of workshops in a series are all adaptable to the needs of the participants and the realities of the setting.
- Encourage collaborative ventures. Involve professionals from the various fields that contribute to the promotion of family literacy— reading specialists, early childhood specialists, adult literacy providers, and children's librarians, among others.
- View literacy in its broadest sense: as all the activities that sup-

port communication, contribute to academic achievement, provide ways to make sense of experience, and afford enjoyment.

- Build evaluation into the program design, but be flexible about methods. Evaluation should be appropriate to the program design and goals. Test scores are often inappropriate measurements for a program of this type. Home reading records, interviews, and observation by outside experts should be used. Look for behavior and attitude changes. If participants say they are reading more, the program is having an important impact. Evaluate the influence on both parent and child.

MOTHEREAD®, INC.

MOTHEREAD®—Steven Gaj, 1989

". . . it will make you feel good inside that you can relate to them [your children], read to them. . . . If you can't relate to them while you're in prison, you can't relate to them when you get out."

—Doris
(prison inmate, mother of four)

"A 1986 study by the National Institute of Corrections (NIC) found that eventually 95 percent of all those in prison return to society, but that a very high percentage—estimates vary, as high as 70 percent—will wind up back in prison within a year of their release. Yet the only factor known to reduce inmate recidivism is the maintenance of family ties."

—Duke Directions
November 1988

Background

At the heart of the MOTHEREAD® program is the belief that the parent-child connection and the desire to preserve and strengthen it are profoundly motivating to the adult learner. By emphasizing the connections among learning, human relationships, and the power of stories, Nancye Gaj, who designed the program, seeks to enable parents to use language in a way that is significant to them, by providing them with a greater understanding of and involvement with their community, their children, and themselves.

MOTHEREAD® was launched in July 1987 under the leadership of Secretary Patric Dorsey of the North Carolina Department of Cultural Resources, who, when approached by Nancye Gaj, shared her vision of offering a reading program to mothers separated from their children by imprisonment. Securing permission from the administration of a maximum-security women's prison in Raleigh and obtaining funding for the pilot year were the two greatest challenges in organizing the program. Secretary Dorsey was largely responsible for securing initial funding for the MOTHEREAD® prison project from the federal volunteer agency ACTION, and for establishing a partnership between the Department of Corrections and the Department of Cultural Resources. Nancye Gaj was responsible for finding staff to assist in the design and teaching of the curriculum, developing a program model, creating public information flyers and brochures, and securing ongoing funding and community links for MOTHEREAD®, Inc., a nonprofit educational organization. One major concern was that the project would run successfully for one year and then fold because of a lack of sustained support. Another was that it would be difficult to create links between the community and a prison project, or to dispel the perception that MOTHEREAD®, Inc. was limited to serving parents in prison. However, since 1987, MOTHEREAD®, Inc. has greatly expanded the scope of their services to both community and prison organizations.

The Program

Setting: There are MOTHEREAD® program sites in women's prisons, libraries, churches, schools, and child-care centers.

Funding

The organization is currently supported by the Z. Smith Reynolds Foundation, the North Carolina Humanities Council, the sponsors of the Greater Greensboro Open, and is an affiliate of the North Carolina Center for Literacy Development. Additional funding is provided by individuals, businesses, service groups, and churches.

Components

- Children's books with stories that share rich yet simple language and powerful illustrations are chosen because they lend themselves to adult discussion. Classes are focused on creating connections between parents and children, capitalizing on the shared history, intimacy, and motivation that make the parent unique as teacher.
- Products created by the program include writings, story-telling audiotapes, and story dramatizations.
- Training for volunteers, administrators, and educators emphasizes learning based on students' strengths rather than weaknesses.
- Training workshops cover topics that include program philosophy, structure, and curriculum; language-teaching strategies that involve students in learner-centered curriculum development and evalua-

tion techniques; how to create community links with a family literacy program; and story sharing and language development in young children.
- MOTHEREAD® teacher's guide (lesson plans and exercises) and "storystretchers" encourage discussions.

Evidence of Success

- Pre- and postinstruction videotapes document changes in parents' self-confidence, progress in reading accurately and effectively, and a new ability to make a story come alive.
- Students report changes in reading behaviors, benefits to their relationships with their children, and changes in their children's attitudes about reading. Examples include using books to open up discussion of ideas and issues, dramatizing books together, children's play being based on stories read, increased letter writing, children requesting books as gifts. Parents progress in skill development, such as reading for the main idea, understanding symbolism, and reading with inflection.
- MOTHEREAD® is currently developing an evaluation process that will enable them to formally document changes in reading behavior as well as in perceptions about reading.

Advice to Policy-Makers and Practitioners

- For literacy programs to work they must be part of an existing social network, or people won't participate. Programs shouldn't be separated from other community activities and services.
- Don't start a family literacy pilot without identifying and talking with prospective students, identifying a class location and teacher, and determining the curriculum content that is appropriate for your prospective students and feasible for your teachers. A family literacy program needs to be grounded in some way, such as through an ongoing funder, community support, or student base.

MOTHERS' READING PROGRAM

Mothers' Reading Program—Sara Schwabacher, 1989

By the time Pat joined the Mothers' Reading Program she was frustrated with her inability to read. Day after day she told stories, the teacher transcribed them, and Pat haltingly read the stories back. But every morning during the first few weeks Pat was unable to read the story she had created the previous day. Then one day she read back the words "holler" and "husband," and that was Pat's breakthrough. "I couldn't believe I read those words," she said. "I secretly thought I was brain damaged and would never read at all . . .

"When I first started back to school my son was ten years old. He would help me with my reading. Up till then the only one of my children who knew I couldn't read was my daughter. I had been ashamed before, but I could see how proud my son was that I was learning and that he could help me. He's proud of me for being in school. He sees me going to school now at my age and it makes him see how important it is for him to get his education now. My being in school has helped him with his own reading. . . ."

—Pat (forty years old,
the first student in
Mothers' Reading Program)

Background

The Mothers' Reading Program was begun by the American Reading Council in 1984.

The American Reading Council had learned firsthand through its reading programs for children that the children who were not reading had mothers who also did not read. Over and over again, in The Friendly Place/El Sitio Simpático, its community learning center in New York City's East Harlem community, in its Open Sesame Language Arts Curriculum in public schools, and in Head Start programs, the council had learned the lesson: In order to break through the wall of illiteracy, teaching reading must be an intergenerational activity.

This knowledge led to the conception of the council's Mothers' Reading Program, which is now in its fifth year. The program seeks to demonstrate that teaching reading to both mothers and children, using a similar approach in the same learning environment, is the road to true literacy—not simply the acquisition of skin-deep, rote skills but a deeply felt sense of the usefulness of literacy and literature that makes reading an ongoing and vital part of daily life.

The Mothers' Reading Program teaches adults to read through group creation of literature. As the world is "read" by participants, through dialogue about events in the community, about reading and not reading, about education, parenting, and the myriad events and issues that affect mothers in present-day New York, the dialogue is transformed into written texts. The texts are in the form of stories, news articles, dialogues, essays, poetry, and plays. This community literature becomes the core reading material and is used to build language skills. From it, students create personal dictionaries and personal diaries using invented spelling and, gradually, mainstream English.

The Program

Setting: For the last two years the Mothers' Reading Program has been located at University Settlement, a one-hundred-year-old settlement house, the first in New York City, in an area of great poverty on Manhattan's Lower East Side. The community is diverse, with large groups of Chinese and of Hispanics from the Caribbean and Central and Latin America. There also is a sizable group of Bengalese, as well as some Vietnamese and other nationalities. When the American Reading Council was approached by the settlement house, their Head Start director, a woman with years of experience in many parts of the country, said, "I have never seen an area with such an acute need for help in literacy."

Funding

The program is supported by the New York City Literacy Initiative (city and state funds) and private funding, including Jurzykowski Foundation, New York Life Foundation, and St. James Church, Madison Avenue.

Components

Parent literacy training: Mothers attend adult literacy courses using a specially designed community literature approach. Students meet in a group class and use text materials developed by the group.

Parenting/parent education: Class-developed text materials often include parenting/parent education content. The Mothers' Reading Program library is stocked with books for children and for parents.

Prereading/language development activities: The Head Start classroom teachers have incorporated the council's Open Sesame Language Arts Curriculum into their programs. This involves extensive reading aloud, an environment filled with reading materials, stories dictated or written by children, and active parent involvement with reading and writing activities.

Other: Literacy training components (text and skill development) are being extended to community projects, such as making the Mothers' Reading Program library a work project for the class, developing a written text into a videotaped "telenovella," and creating collaborative projects with neighboring community agencies, including the Henry Street Settlement Arts for Living Center.

Evidence of Success

- Frequent and extensive borrowing of books from the Mothers' Reading Program library by children and parents.
- Parent involvement in Head Start activities.
- Publication of four volumes of selected writings by the students.
- Parent grade-level advancement on standardized reading tests.

Advice to Policy-Makers and Practitioners

- All you need to generate a good literacy program is a group of learners and a teacher trained to explore their concerns, who can, with those learners, transform their needs into reading materials.
- Any place where students or parents are already gathered—a school, a community center, a union, a church, a workplace—can become a learning center.
- Administrators of the host site for the program must understand and support the endeavor.

ARKANSAS HOME INSTRUCTION PROGRAM FOR PRESCHOOL YOUNGSTERS (HIPPY)

HIPPY—Rae Ann Fields, 1988

"I always knew I could feed and clothe my son, but I never tried to teach him anything because I thought anything I taught him would be wrong."

—HIPPY Parent

Background

The Home Instruction Program was developed in 1969 by a team headed by Dr. Avima D. Lombard at the NCJW Research Institute for Innovation in Education, at Hebrew University in Jerusalem, Israel. Initiated as a research project, it was designed to examine the feasibility and effect of home-based educational intervention involving mothers and their pre-school children from educationally disadvantaged sectors of the country. The goal was to prepare immigrant children to enter the highly competitive Israeli education system. In 1975, the project passed from the research phase to the operational phase on a country-wide basis, and today, almost twenty years later, it serves approximately 13,000 families yearly in more than 110 urban and rural communities. It also exists in five other countries and seven American states. While it is funded by the Israeli Ministry of Education and Culture, Hebrew University maintains control over the implementation and coordination of the program.

HIPPY came to America in 1982 virtually unchanged. The following events helped to shape the Arkansas HIPPY experience:

- September 1985: Hillary Rodham Clinton, first lady of Arkansas, read about HIPPY in the *Miami Herald* and decided to investigate the prospects of bringing it to Arkansas.
- February 1986: Following five months of study and exploration, the governor's office, in partnership with two state agencies, sponsored a one-day conference introducing HIPPY to state educators and community leaders.
- June 1986: Four women from Arkansas went to Israel to the HIPPY International Workshop.
- September 1986: The first four pilot programs began in Little Rock, Pulaski County, Russellville, and Pine Bluff.
- April 1987: As the first year drew to a close, another conference

was held to invite interested parties to see how the program was doing. Following this conference, six more Arkansans attended the next HIPPY International Workshop, and as a result, six additional programs began in the state in September 1987.

- June 1988: Four more Arkansans went to Israel as four new programs were developed. Currently, as the 1988–89 school year ends, there are fourteen sites in twenty-three Arkansas counties, with expectations of more programs to begin in September 1989.

The Program

Setting: A unique feature of the HIPPY program is the fact that it is home-based rather than located at a site outside the home. Twice a month a paraprofessional, who must also be a mother or father from the same community, visits the parent and works with him or her on weekly lessons. On alternating weeks the parents gather for group meetings. Currently there are seven programs in public school districts, six that are based in community centers, YWCAs and community action agencies, and one that is run through a state educational cooperative.

Funding

The program is currently funded through the Job Training Partnership Act (Chapters I and II) Planning and Development money from the Department of Vocational Education, Save the Children Federation, and the Winthrop Rockefeller Foundation.

Components

- The instructional program consists of packets of programmed material that concentrate on language, discrimination skills, and problem solving. The degree of difficulty increases throughout the two-year period.
- Language instruction is carried out using storybooks given to the families. Parents learn how to ask questions about details of content, vocabulary, and concepts.
- Daily worksheets track the lessons from the stories. The work-sheets serve as guides for sensory-discrimination skills by offering visual, auditory, and tactile exercises. Problem-solving exercises require the child to list, sort, match, and group attributes and ideas.
- Parents are required to work with their children fifteen minutes a

day, five days a week, thirty weeks annually for two years, the second of which is the year the child is in kindergarten.

The parent is trained by a paraprofessional from the same community who also has a four-year-old in HIPPY. The paraprofessional visits the home every other week.

Twice a month the mothers and fathers gather for group meetings with their paraprofessionals to receive the next week's lesson, and also to learn to interact with other parents in the program. They share their experiences, talk about their problems, reinforce their goals, and lend one another support. In-service programs covering subjects such as health, safety, and citizenship are also provided.

Each program has one coordinator for every twelve paraprofessionals. Each paraprofessional works with ten to fifteen families.

Evidence of Success

- Tests administered to both parents and children before and after the program indicate gains. For example, in the fall of 1986, 6 percent of the children in one district entering HIPPY tested average and none tested above average. In the spring of 1988, 74 percent of the children in the second year of the program tested average or above.
- The program has been replicated around the state.
- HIPPY parents are asking for more literacy help, going back to school, and seeking employment. They are registering to vote.
- Parents are more involved in their children's school work and are more apt to provide necessary school supplies, such as paper and books.

Advice to Policy-Makers and Practitioners

"When we first began studying HIPPY in Arkansas, emphasis was on the child. If the child did well, then the mother would enjoy a feeling of success. Now, in Arkansas and throughout the nation where HIPPY is being implemented, the focus appears to be shifting toward the mother's growth. If we are able to give her a program where she can teach her child and make a positive contribution to his or her education, if we can help her realize the possibilities of growth within herself, if we can open doors for her that have never been open for her, then we have helped not only her and her child but the entire family."

—Ann Kamps, Special Assistant
for Early Childhood Programs

PARENTS AS PARTNERS IN READING:
A FAMILY LITERACY PROGRAM FOR TEACHERS AND ADMINISTRATORS

Parents as Partners—Alice Flanagan, 1989

"Mr. Chairman and members of the Committee, I hope you had the opportunity to read the February 21 article in the Washington Post *which described the parent involvement program I developed in Donaldsonville, Louisiana. You perhaps noticed that I used a Saturday night and Sunday morning approach for recruiting poor and minority parents for the Parents as Partners in Reading program. I enlisted two of the most important community leaders: Ray Jacobs, owner of a popular Donaldsonville tavern, Jonelle's, and the Rev. William D. Hogan of St. Catherine's, a predominantly black Roman Catholic church. These people were not the mayor, the rotary club president, or the school resource people. They were the natural leaders of the community I was trying to tap.*

"Ray Jacobs started telling mothers who patronized his tavern that they no longer would be welcome unless they put as much time into learning how to read to their children as they spent enjoying themselves at his tavern. He took his commitment one step further, driving parents to the weekly Parents as Partners class and participating himself.

"Father Hogan, who has served black Catholics during his entire thirty-seven-year career, preached about the benefits of the Parents as Partners program during his Sunday sermons. His message was that literacy is an important tool of faith."

—Patricia A. Edwards
Hearing Before the Select Subcommittee on
Education of the House
Committee on Education and Labor
March 9, 1989

Background

Parents as Partners in Reading is the brainchild of Dr. Patricia A. Edwards, a Louisiana State University professor of education. The program seeks to improve the literacy rate among socioeconomically deprived families by teaching parents how to read to their children—something that does not come naturally to those who are not brought up in environments that promote literacy.

The idea for the program began to germinate several years ago as

40

a result of a reading study Dr. Edwards had conducted at a Head Start center in Louisiana. In order to study the book-reading techniques of these parents, she videotaped five mothers reading to their children and observed the following:

- The first mother painstakingly read the book word by word and struggled to get through the text.
- The second was a teenage mother, and she asked in the middle of the videotape, "What do I do, do I point to the pictures? Do I ask questions? What do I do?"
- The third mother quickly read the book without stopping and said, "The end."
- The fourth mother read with two preschool sons but hurriedly moved the book from one child to the other until neither child was able to get anything from the book.
- The fifth mother spanked her child in frustration.

Dr. Edwards showed this videotape to a group of kindergarten and first-grade teachers, who were shocked. As the tape clearly demonstrated, "Reading is not a literacy event in every family's home and books are not a literacy artifact."

When she moved to Louisiana State University, she wanted to continue her research on parent/child book reading, but she knew she needed to do something else. She also knew that it was imperative for her to help teachers to understand that they needed to move from "telling" to "showing" parents what "read to your child" meant.

So, in the fall of 1987, at the request of the Ascension Parish school system she established the Parents as Partners in Reading program in Donaldsonville, a town of eight thousand residents about twenty-five miles down the Mississippi River from the Baton Rouge campus. The participation and support of key community members have been significant factors in the program's success.

The Program

Setting: The program takes place in the elementary school library in Donaldsonville, Louisiana, and is currently being replicated at Withrow School in Springfield, Illinois.

Funding

During the 1987–88 school year, Dr. Edwards received a $500 minigrant from the Louisiana State Reading Association and a $4,000 faculty research grant from Louisiana State University. The second school year (1988–89), she received a $10,560 grant from the Ascension Parish School Board (Donaldsonville, Louisiana); however, there is significant material support from the community.

Components

- Viewing of videotapes of outstanding teachers and project staff modeling exemplary book-reading behaviors;
- Ongoing creation of videotapes of program parents reading to their children;
- Identification of and training in successful reading behaviors. Successful behaviors include connecting book information with what children already know, asking questions about sequencing of events and facts in a story, making comparisons and developing other thinking skills;
- Identifying areas needing improvement, in a positive way, and improving them;
- Lending parents books from school library to facilitate practice at home;
- Reviewing all tapes before summer recess.

The program takes place over the entire school year, for two hours each week, beginning in August and ending in May.

Evidence of Success

- By viewing before and after videotapes of the parents reading to their children, significant differences in the parents' ability to share books with their young children can be observed.
- Teachers have reported an improvement in student achievement in the elementary school.
- Parents have reported that book reading has become an integral part of their daily lives.
- Teacher morale has improved because of better communication with parents.
- The community values and participates in the program: community leaders helped recruit parents; the school board hired a bus driver to provide transportation for the parents; the principal invited parents to eat lunch with their children; the school librarian allowed parents to check out books under their children's names. Enrollment grew from twenty-five parents in the 1987–88 school year to ninety-five parents in the 1988–89 year.

Advice to Policy-Makers
and Practitioners

- Build a unified effort that links home, school, and community. Let people know they can make a difference in the school system.
- More research is needed. Once the research is done, it needs to be disseminated and written in a manner that school administrators, teachers, parents, and community leaders can understand.

PARENT LEADERSHIP TRAINING PROJECT

Parent Leadership—Catherine Watters, 1989

"What is special about this program in Washington is that it shows that even if you can't speak English, it doesn't mean you can't participate in your child's education."

—Lisa Contini-Seguin, Producer,
Project Literacy U.S. (PLUS) at WQED,
the *Grandview Herald* (Wash.), 2/21/89

Background

The Parent Leadership Training Project is a pilot program begun in 1986, and conducted by Citizens' Education Center Northwest in cooperation with the Washington State Migrant Council. The council invited the center to work with Chicano/Latino parents in Sunnyside, Washington. It is estimated that as many as 86 percent of the children of families working in the Yakima Valley (the project location) drop out of school before graduation, some as early as seventh or eighth grade. The project is designed to help parents and children make a successful transition from preschool to public school kindergarten by early involvement of the parents in the education of their children, thereby helping to lower that extremely high percentage of drop-outs.

The Program

Setting: Project sites are located at Washington State Migrant Council Preschool Centers in Sunnyside and Mabton and in Wapato and Toppenish school districts. The project has recently been replicated at an elementary school in Seattle.

Funding

The project is supported by individuals, corporations, and foundations, including the Fred Meyer Charitable Trust and the John D. and Catherine T. MacArthur Foundation.

Components

The project provides a series of fourteen parent-training sessions. Teachers, principals and other administrators are invited. Child care and refreshments are provided. Topics include:

- Information on what children learned in preschool and how to build on and reinforce those skills during the summer prior to entering kindergarten;
- Rights and responsibilities of parents;
- Student testing;
- Parent-teacher relations;
- How to help a child at home during the school years;
- How to deal with children's problems in school before they become intractable;
- How to read a report card;
- How to help their children read even if the parent can't, using wordless books to model effective ways a parent can "read" to his or her child.

For example, J. Garcia had no formal education and felt she had nothing to contribute to her children. With wordless books, she could sit down with her child, have him "read" a story he made up, and begin a discussion about it. They discussed what reading was, stopped periodically to explore what might happen, plotted endings, and engaged in other important prereading activities.

English-as-a-second-language (ESL) classes provided by other community agencies are an additional component.

Evidence of Success

- Project has been replicated with parents of children in grades K–5.
- Parents are reading or having someone read to their children at home on a regular basis.
- Parents are visiting libraries.
- Parents are involved in their children's schoolwork.

Advice to Policy-Makers and Practitioners

- Get cooperation from those interested in having the project implemented—from the top down. If the project is in a school district, start with the superintendent, then approach the school

building principal, staff, home visitors, and federal-program directors.
- Make sure everything is understood up front, in terms of recruitment, advertising, child-care providers.
- Make sure the people you work with are committed to the project.

AVANCE FAMILY SUPPORT AND EDUCATION PROGRAM

Avance—Bruce Deuley, 1989

"Every young child counts—we cannot afford to lose one to poverty and lack of education. We should all have a vested interest in our children.

"The most effective way to help our children is through the most fundamental and basic unit of society, the family. Family support programs which are located where the families are—in the communities; which are comprehensive in scope; which are preventive in nature will give these children a better opportunity to become productive, contributing members of society and allow them to partake of the fruits that this country has to offer."

—Gloria Rodriguez
from the *San Antonio Light*
January 1988

Background

In 1973, the Avance Parent-Child Education Program was established to reduce the disproportionately high dropout rate among the Mexican-American community on the west side of San Antonio. The founder, Gloria Rodriguez, became interested and involved in parenting education and support because of her own experiences coming from a poor but strong, nurturing family, and from her experiences as a former schoolteacher of first-grade children who seemed destined to fail because they entered school so ill-prepared. The program is designed to help children do well in school by teaching parents to teach their children and by meeting the needs of the parents.

Avance, which means advancement or progress in Spanish, was modeled after the former Parent-Child Development Centers, funded by the Department of Health, Education, and Welfare, Office of Child Development, Administration for Children, Youth, and Families. With a grant from the Zale Foundation, the first Avance Center opened in the Mirasol Federal Housing Project in San Antonio, Texas. The latest, and fourth, site was opened in 1987 and is also located within a housing project.

The adult basic education and advanced education component was added in 1981. This was later to be known as the Avance Adult Literacy Program.

The Program

Setting: Avance has established programs in public housing projects, converted day-care centers, churches, and diverse community centers.

Funding

The program is supported by the city of San Antonio, United Way, Texas Department of Human Services, private foundations, and individual contributions.

Components

Parenting/parent education

- Community-based workshops develop parenting skills, strengthen the family unit, and build the home/school relationship.
- The Fatherhood Project involves husbands in the program in family-strengthening activities.
- A homebound parenting education program and a support program for abusive parents with young children are offered.
- Basic literacy and advanced education provides educational opportunities for families who have successfully completed the parenting program, and for individuals from the community at large.

Prereading/language development activities

- Classes teach the basic concepts and skills necessary for success in school, as well as those needed for the child's language development.
- Introduction and access to the library.
- Instruction for parents in how to develop their own books at home.

Other

- Toy-making activities.
- Home visits reinforce what is learned in class.
- Videotapes for self-critiques.
- Community resource awareness and utilization activities.

Evidence of Success

- Enrollment of parents in adult education programs.
- Increased value of education to parents.
- Greater parental expectations of children's school achievement.
- Greater utilization of community resources.
- Increased involvement of parents in school activities.
- The program is currently undergoing an intensive three-year $750,000 evaluation and research study sponsored by the Carnegie Corporation of New York. The purpose is to document what works, for whom it works, and why.

Advice to Policy-Makers and Practitioners

- Policy-makers, business leaders, and practitioners of successful family literacy programs need to discuss what we have learned thus far in supporting low-income, high-risk families and how other industrialized nations support the family.
- Components of successful intervention models need to be incorporated into institutions at the community level.
- Services to families must begin in the home, be community-based, comprehensive in scope, preventive in nature, and have children (ages three and under) as the entry point to child and parent.
- Definitions of the roles of local government and other funding institutions as well as the providers of services need to be clearly stated to best serve the people.
- We don't have to reinvent the wheel. We need to utilize the expertise of those who have been successfully serving hard-to-reach families.
- Programs offering services to families need to be adequately funded, adequately staffed, and run like a business, with sensitive and dedicated personnel, who know the people, their problems and culture.
- All families need support—especially the fastest-growing minority groups with the lowest educational and income levels.
- Practitioners should clearly understand the community problems and the organization's mission. They must be able to demonstrate that the services they offer are making a significant difference. Money for evaluation must be made available.

Program Summary Chart

PROGRAM SUMMARY CHART

PROGRAM	GOALS	TARGET POPULATION	OUTREACH	FUNDING
PACE	• To help adults acquire basic skills, child-care skills, and high school equivalency certificate • To improve parents' attitudes toward education • To promote active involvement of parent in child's preschool education • To prepare preschool youngsters for success by developing learning skills	• Parents lacking a high school diploma who have 3- or 4-year-old children	• Information provided through community groups, organizations, & social service agencies • Use of posted information, print & visual media statewide • Use recruitment by program participants to attract family members & friends	• State-financed in its entirety • Support in kind from local districts with transportation, classroom space & administrative services
Kenan	• To encourage the active role of parents as "first teachers" • To improve the nurturing relationship of parent and child • To prepare parents as educational role models for their children • To increase developmental skills of preschool children • To integrate parents into the school setting	• Parents, guardians, or caregivers who do not have a high school diploma, and who have 3- or 4-year-old children	• Home visits with known prospects • Use of electronic & print public-service announcements • Presentation to social service agencies • Brochures, flyers, and newsletters • Word of mouth, peer recruitment	• Private foundation • State education & human resource agencies

SUPPORT SERVICES	MATERIALS	SPECIAL FEATURES	OUTCOMES
• Transportation and meals provided for parents & children • Stipend provided to program-completers to purchase children's educational materials for home use	*For Adults* • Individualized curricula using texts based on diagnostic prescription of skills needed • Parental instruction adapted from nationally validated curriculum *For Children* • Nationally validated, cognitively oriented early childhood curriculum	• Parents & children attend classes together in public school setting • Programs operate under direct supervision of public schools • Early childhood training & curricula provide a consistent model for trainers, teachers, & parents	• Measures of academic gain show adults achieving educational goals (GEDs) and raising basic skill levels significantly • Adults enrolling in further education or job training • Anecdotal evidence from classrooms shows teachers that PACE children are better prepared for school success than non-PACE children
• Transportation and meals provided • Screening evaluations for children to test hearing and speech • Stipend provided to parents with high attendance records to purchase educational materials for children • Transportation provided for parents to attend school activities	*For Adults* • Basal Adult Education texts • High school equivalency test preparation texts *For Children* • Cognitively oriented, early childhood developmental curriculum • Manipulables, toys, and play furniture	• Contextual learning & teaching within family • Comprehensive array of services to serve needs of adults & children • Emphasis on staff development activities to enable staff to act as team • Staff trained in all components of program	• Through extensive interviews & staff anecdotal records parents report gain in independent functioning & greater sense of control over their lives • Adults at relatively high skills levels able to meet their educational levels • Children demonstrated marked improvements in language, independence, decision-making, and pre-academic performance

(continued)

PROGRAM	GOALS	TARGET POPULATION	OUTREACH	FUNDING
SER Family Learning Centers	• To provide youths & adults with basic skills they need to succeed in world of work • To provide preschool youth with educational headstart • To enable Hispanic parents to play a significant role in their children's formal education.	• Low income, "at risk" youth & adults, primarily from minority (Hispanic, Black, and Asian) population groups • Children ages 2–5 years old	• Use of electronic & print media for public-service announcements • Promotion of programs through network of community organizations • Posters & program information circulated in businesses, schools, and churches	• Foundations • Corporations • Individual contributors • Grants from federal agencies • Private industry councils (PICs) support through Job Training Partnership
Parent Readers	• To improve reading skills & practices of adults through reading & discussion of children's literature • To improve literacy environment of the home by increasing literacy skills of adults & children	• Disadvantaged community-college students enrolled in remedial reading classes who are parents (or adults interested in forming a reading relationship with a child) • Children served indirectly, ages 6 months to 13 years	• Recruitment of parents in remedial reading classes by: – Staff visits and presentations to classes, soliciting interest – Follow-up letters to interested students – Phone calls and reminders precede workshop and further explain program – Peer recruitment by students in program	• Foundation grants • Research awards from technical college • Donations of books from publishing companies

SUPPORT SERVICES	MATERIALS	SPECIAL FEATURES	OUTCOMES
Child care In some sites, transportation, medical and dental exams	*For Parents* • Computer-assisted instruction, videotapes, and commercial texts *For Children* • Interactive video, computer-based reading program & manipulables, read-along cassette tapes	• Use of technology in self-paced automated learning systems • Multigenerational instruction program	• Evidence gained through interviews, attitude assessments, and participant evaluations reveals: – More adults active in children's education – Parents monitor children's homework and study time – Parents motivated to learn more to stay abreast of children's educational development
Participants borrow books, and children receive books as gifts	*For Parents & Children* • Contemporary children's literature & classics • Fiction: fables, folktales, poetry • Nonfiction: science, history, & other cultures • Range from wordless picture books to books with great deal of text *For Adults* • Selections that parallel topics for children (folktales, poetry) and wide range of authors	• Population served — community-college students • Parents "positioned" to make a difference in children's educational development • Program is research-based • Use of children's literature as instructional material linking student and parent role • Adaptable to a variety of settings & populations	• Case study interviews & self-reporting parent surveys reveal: – Improvement in literacy environment of the home – Parents involving children in reading activities – Parents becoming literacy resources to their children, providing more materials for reading – More parental involvement in child's schooling

(continued)

PROGRAM	GOALS	TARGET POPULATION	OUTREACH	FUNDING
MOTHEREAD®	• To enable parents with low literacy skills to serve as reading role models for their children • To create awareness of dramatic play, storytelling, and personal expression as critical elements in literacy development for adults & children	• Parents who are under stress as single parents, victims of alcohol or drug abuse, parents with children ages 2–10	• Advocacy of program by word of mouth • Incentives offered within prison (including visitation & time off release dates) • Presentations and publicity in local print & electronic media	• Public & private foundations • Professional advocacy group • Federal agency • Community literacy coalitions & other organizations • Individual donations
Mothers' Reading	• To increase parents' ability to help their children become readers • To assist nonreading parents in developing basic literacy skills • To develop a student-run library for children & parents	• Low-income mothers with children in Head Start program who also have low level reading skills (children ages 3–4)	• Head Start parents recruited through program orientation • Referrals from city clearinghouse • Program information provided by social services staff	• Foundations • Public agencies (city & state) • Support of private community organizations (churches) • Community in-kind donations

SUPPORT SERVICES	MATERIALS	SPECIAL FEATURES	OUTCOMES
• Children's books	*For Adults* • Audiotapes for storytelling • Children's literature, related poetry & pieces — adult writing *For Children* • Children's literature	• Prison/correctional setting • Learner-centered instruction tailored to meet a specific goal • Participatory curriculum development • Designed to help parents stay in touch with their children while parent is incarcerated	• Through teacher observation & student reports & videotaped sessions, results noted include: – Strengthened relationships between parents and children – Increased reading comprehension skills – Increased communication between parents and children – Children's increased interest in books – Adults pursue further education or enroll in vocational program
• Child care & meals provided • Pre-employment training • Transportation (carfare)	*For Parents* • Text materials created by adult students • High interest/low difficulty texts *For Children* • Children's literature	• Development of community literature • Coordination between Head Start (Early Childhood) and adult literacy approaches • Student-run library as resource for parents & children & as job skill experience	Activities of program participants reveal: – Extensive borrowing of books by children and parents – Parental involvement in Head Start activities – Development of reading program texts for literacy instruction

(continued)

PROGRAM	GOALS	TARGET POPULATION	OUTREACH	FUNDING
HIPPY	• To provide home-based mutual learning experiences for parents & children • To prepare preschool-aged children for better success in formal education • To motivate parents to act as their children's teachers	• Educationally at-risk 4- and 5-year-old children and their families • Majority of families economically disadvantaged	• Neighborhood canvassing • Use of community agencies and private organizations • Advertising in print & electronic media • Referrals from other parents • Announcements through schools & Head Start programs	• Foundations • Federal programs (JTPA), Vocational Education Compensatory Education (Chapter I & Chapter II) • Community in-kind donations
Parents as Partners	• To increase parental involvement in schooling of their children • To improve parents' ability to read to their children • To broaden community support involvement in parent-child programs • To improve communication between parents, teachers & school administrators	• Parents whose kindergarten, 1st, 2nd, & 3rd grade children deemed at risk by teachers	• School administrators active in program promotion • Parents invited to orientation, then become peer recruiters • Key community leaders personally involved	• Professional foundation grant • Local school board • State university research grants

SUPPORT SERVICES	MATERIALS	SPECIAL FEATURES	OUTCOMES
• In some sites, lending libraries, transportation, and child care	*For Parents* • Instructional worksheets *For Children* • Story books, manipulables	• Emphasis on parent as teacher, providing direct instruction to child • Support system for parent that provides encouragement & instills confidence	• Through parent inventories, results indicate: – Parents seeking additional education & employment opportunities – Parents more involved in children's schoolwork – Adults becoming more active in school and community affairs • Evaluation includes before-and-after literacy testing for children, and for adults in some sites
• Transportation and meals provided • Use of school library for parents to check out children's books	*For Parents* • Videotapes of effective book reading interactions • Taped sessions of program participants reading to their children *For Children* • Picture books, story books, concept books • Literature from library (easy-to-read books)	• Community support in recruitment, transportation, and promoting value of program activities • Strong support from school administration • Parents shown how to be effective in reading to their children through use of videotaped parent-child sessions	• Use of videotape & teacher anecdotal reports & parent comments reveal: – Improvement in parents' ability to share books with their children – Teacher reports of improvement in student achievement – Book reading as integral part of daily parent-child activities

(continued)

PROGRAM	GOALS	TARGET POPULATION	OUTREACH	FUNDING
Parent Leadership Training	• To help parents become more active in their children's education • To provide parents with information & strategies for helping children at home • To assist parents in learning about schools' functions • To enable parents to communicate with school personnel	• Hispanic migrant farmworkers and their children (ages 4–10)	• Home visits • Phone calls to parents • Flyers and notices about weekly sessions • Monthly radio program	• Private foundations
Avance Family Support & Education	• To improve parental knowledge, attitudes, & skills in the growth & development of children • To strengthen the family unit and home/school relationship • To provide educational opportunities leading to greater self-sufficiency	• Low-income parents & their children (ages birth–3 years old)	• Door-to-door solicitation • Public service announcements, flyers, use of newspapers • Word of mouth	• Foundations • City & state agency support • Individual contributions • Nonprofit community organizations

SUPPORT SERVICES	MATERIALS	SPECIAL FEATURES	OUTCOMES
• Child care • Wordless picture books provided	*For Adults & Children* • Materials developed by program include information from class sessions and home activities	• Series of sessions with follow-up hands-on activities for home use • Assistance to parents as children enter public school • Parents act as a support group for one another	• Interviews with program participants suggest: – Parents beginning to read or have someone read to their children on a regular basis – Parents visiting libraries more often – Parents using wordless books supplied by program
• Child care • Meals for children • Nutrition classes for parents • Referral services • Toy-lending library • Food bank	*For Parents* • Parenting education curriculum • Toymaking manual • Commercial texts in basic skills *For Children* • Commercial early childhood curriculum	• Community-based program • Services delivered simultaneously to parents & children	• Adults enrolled in programs have, as a result: – Enrolled in adult-education programs – Become more involved in children's schooling – Demonstrated greater awareness of importance of education – Increased expectations for children's achievement in school

PROGRAM CONTACTS

Parent and Child Education (PACE) Program
Jeanne Heberle, PACE Coordinator
Division of Community Instruction
Kentucky Department of Education
Capital Plaza Tower
Frankfort, KY 40601
(502) 564-3921

The Kenan Trust Family Literacy Project
Sharon Darling, President
National Center for Family Literacy
One Riverfront Plaza, Suite 608
Louisville, KY 40202
(502) 584-1133

SER Family Learning Centers (FLCs) of SER-Jobs for Progress, Inc.
Ms. Allison Parker
SER National Communications Office
SER-Jobs for Progress National, Inc.
1355 River Bend Drive, Suite 240
Dallas, TX 75247
(214) 631-3999

Parent Readers Program
Ellen Goldsmith, Ed.D.
Parent Readers Program
New York City Technical College
300 Jay Street
Brooklyn, NY 11201
(718) 643-5723

Motheread®, Inc.
Nancye Gaj
MOTHEREAD®, Inc.
P.O. Box 6434
Raleigh, NC 27628
(919) 781-2088; 781-2140

Mothers' Reading Program
Maritza Arrastia
Mothers' Reading Program
c/o University Settlement
184 Eldridge Street
New York, NY 10002
(212) 674-9120 Ext. 176

Julia R. Palmer
American Reading Council
45 John Street
New York, NY 10038
(212) 619–6044

Arkansas Home Instruction Program for Preschool Youngsters (HIPPY)
Ann Kamps, Special Assistant for
  Early Childhood Programs
Office of the Governor
State Capitol Building, Suite 205
Little Rock, AR 72201
(501) 682-2345

Parents as Partners in Reading
Patricia A. Edwards, Ph.D.
College of Education, Erickson Hall
Michigan State University
East Lansing, MI 48823
(517) 355–9628

Parent Leadership Training Project
Dalia Candanoza, Coordinator
Citizens Education Center Northwest
c/o Project Success
312 Division
Grandview, WA 98930
(509) 882-5800

Avance Family Support and Education Program
Mrs. Gloria G. Rodriguez
Executive Director
301 South Frio Road
San Antonio, TX 78207
(512) 270-4630

Additional Sources
of Information and Assistance

Applied Behavioral & Cognitive Sciences, Inc. (ABC)
2841 Canon Street
San Diego, CA 92106
Contact: Thomas G. Sticht

Funded by the MacArthur Foundation, ABC has published a thought-provoking booklet entitled *Making the Nation Smarter: The Intergenerational Transfer of Cognitive Ability.*

Collaborations for Literacy (CFL)
Institute for Responsive Education
Boston University
605 Commonwealth Avenue
Boston, MA 02215
Contact: Ruth Nickse

Collaborations for Literacy (CFL), one of the pioneers in intergenerational literacy programs, closed in August 1988; however, a tutor handbook and administrator's manual are still available, as is program-evaluation data from the developer, Dr. Ruth Nickse, who is also the author of an extremely informative paper, "The Noises of Literacy: An Overview of Intergenerational and Family Literacy Programs."

English Family Literacy Project
Bilingual/ESL Studies Program
University of Massachusetts at Boston
Boston, MA 02125-3393
Contact: Elsa Auerbach

The English Family Literacy Project of the University of Massachusetts at Boston is a three-year program funded by Title VII of the Office of Bilingual Education and Minority Language Affairs. In addition to its instructional activities, the project has compiled a unique annotated bibliography of the literature relevant to family literacy for ESL students.

Harvard Family Research Project
Longfellow Hall
Harvard Graduate School of Education
Appian Way
Cambridge, MA 02138
Contact: Heather Weiss

The Harvard Family Research Project conducts research into family support and education programs that provide services to enhance child, adult, and family development. The project disseminates information about state, family support, and education initiatives and policies; about the effectiveness and evaluation of these programs; and about the development of programs in different public and private agencies. A national resource guide to public school affiliated programs, which includes descriptions of some family literacy programs, will be published in late 1989.

Head Start Bureau
P.O. Box 1182
Washington, DC 20013
Contact: Jim O'Brien

The Head Start Program, administered by the Department of Health and Human Services, has provided comprehensive child-development services to low-income families for twenty-five years. Over the past five years, a special emphasis has been placed on promoting literacy and basic education for the parents of the children in the program as well. In October 1988, Head Start and Literacy Volunteers of America initiated a joint family literacy project. Local LVA affiliates train tutors in twenty-four sites in New York and New Jersey and match them with parents of children in Head Start programs who have reading difficulties. Local Head Start programs mobilize and coordinate services, such as transportation, referral, and other social services, to facilitate the literacy training.

International Reading Association (IRA)
800 Barksdale Road
P.O. Box 8139
Newark, DE 19714
Contact: Patricia Dubois

The goals of the International Reading Association are to improve reading, reading education, and literacy. Among its many activities the organization publishes *Family Focus: Reading and Learning Together*, a guide for parents of children in grades K–3, which includes activities and suggestions for parents to use in working with their children. IRA also publishes brochures for parents about their children's reading.

Laubach Literacy Action (LLA)
1320 Jamesville Avenue
P.O. Box 131
Syracuse, NY 13210
Contact: Peter Waite

Laubach Literacy Action is the largest network of private adult literacy programs providing instruction through trained volunteers. New Readers Press, the publishing division of Laubach Literacy International, is planning a book entitled *Family Literacy in Action*, which will introduce readers to a number of family or intergenerational literacy programs established around the country.

Literacy Volunteers of America, Inc. (LVA)
5795 Widewaters Parkway
Syracuse, NY 13214
Contact: Helen "Jinx" Crouch

Literacy Volunteers of America has more than two hundred affiliates throughout the nation working to teach adults to read and to train tutors. *Reading with Children*, a module developed by LVA, includes a videotape, a trainer's guide, and a tutor's handbook. The purpose of the module is to train tutors to use children's literature with parents and other caretakers to develop their reading and writing skills through use of assisted reading, recorded books, writing, puppets, and other supports for story-telling.

National Center for Family Literacy
One Riverfront Plaza, Suite 608
Louisville, KY 40202
Contact: Sharon Darling

The National Center for Family Literacy is a private, nonprofit corporation developed with a grant from the William R. Kenan, Jr. Charitable Trust and established for the purpose of expanding the efforts to solve the nation's literacy problems through family literacy programs. The center will accomplish its purpose by providing free training and technical assistance to program providers; funding selected program models; and disseminating information to literacy providers, federal, state, and local policy-makers, and selected organizations. In addition, the Kenan Family Literacy Program is administered by the center.

Push Literacy Action Now, Inc. (PLAN)
1332 G Street, SE
Washington, DC 20003
Contact: Mike Fox

PLAN is a private, nonprofit voluntary adult literacy program in the District of Columbia. The organization publishes *The Ladder,* a national literacy newsletter. PLAN offers special literacy training for parents through its community-oriented literacy training and advocacy program. *Take Up Reading Now* (TURN), the family literacy model developed by PLAN, includes three program strands: awareness building, advocacy for children's educational rights, and developing access to books and other learning resources. Their family literacy kit, *Laying the Foundations*, includes guidelines for creating a parent-child curriculum and resource materials for trainers and tutors and is available from PLAN.

U.S. Department of Education:

- Clearinghouse on Adult Education
  U.S. Department of Education
  Division of Adult Education
  Mary E. Switzer Building
  400 Maryland Avenue, SW
  Washington, DC 20202

  The clearinghouse, maintained by the Division of Adult Education, offers free information on family literacy. Publications available include fact sheets, descriptions of family literacy programs, and bibliographies.

- Even Start Program
  Compensatory Education Programs
  U.S. Department of Education
  400 Maryland Avenue, SW
  Room 2043
  Washington, DC 20202
  Contact: Thomas W. Fagan

The family-centered education projects funded under the Even Start Program are designed to help parents become partners in the education of their children and at the same time to provide literacy instruction to the parents. Local school districts in all states are eligible to apply for funds.

- Family English Literacy Programs
  Office of Bilingual Education and Minority Language Affairs
  U.S. Department of Education
  400 Maryland Avenue, SW
  Room 5620
  Washington, DC 20202
  Contact: Dr. Mary T. Mahony

The program offers assistance to help adults with limited proficiency in English achieve competence in the English language, and provides instruction on how parents and family members can facilitate the educational achievement of their children. Organizations eligible for assistance are local school districts, colleges and universities, and private nonprofit groups. In 1988, there were thirty-five projects funded by this program.

- Library Literacy Program
  Office of Library Programs
  U.S. Department of Education
  555 New Jersey Avenue, NW
  Suite 400
  Washington, DC 20208
  Contact: Anne Matthews

The Library Literacy Program makes grants to state and local public libraries to support literacy programs. In fiscal year 1988, 224 library literacy projects were funded and 5 percent (or eleven of these projects) provided family literacy activities. A variety of approaches to family literacy are represented in the library literacy projects linking libraries with parents and children in several states. State and local public libraries are eligible to apply for funds.